D0241354

SOD
CALM
AND
GET
ANGRY

For Annette and Kay

SOD CALM AND GET ANGRY

RESIGNED ADVICE FOR HARD TIMES

EBURY
PRESS

13

First published in 2010 by Ebury Press, an imprint of Ebury Publishing
A Random House Group company

Compilation copyright © Ebury Press 2010

The Random House Group Limited Reg. No. 954009

Addresses for companies within the Random House Group can be found
at www.randomhouse.co.uk

A CIP catalogue record for this book is available from the British Library

The Random House Group Limited supports The Forest Stewardship
Council (FSC), the leading international forest certification organisation.
All our titles that are printed on Greenpeace approved FSC certified
paper carry the FSC logo. Our paper procurement policy can be
found at www.rbooks.co.uk/environment

Designed and set by seagulls.net

Printed in Germany by GGP Media GmbH, Pössneck

ISBN 9780091938703

To buy books by your favourite authors and register for offers visit
www.rbooks.co.uk

IF WE SEE LIGHT AT THE END OF THE TUNNEL, IT IS THE LIGHT OF THE ONCOMING TRAIN.

Robert Lowell

CONTENTS

INTRODUCTION

Civilisation

Happiness

Unhappiness

Deceit

Hypocrisy

Morality

Rat Race

Curmudgeon

Anger

Protest

INTRODUCTION

While the celebrated characteristics of 'stiff upper lip' and 'mustn't grumble' are those which first come to mind when we think of our brave island nation in times of crisis, there are always those *other* great British traits not too far behind: disgruntled grumpiness, whispered complaint and incensed anger. 'This is ridiculous', 'I'd like to speak to the manager' and 'We're all going to hell in a handcart' are the traditional battle cries. And in our current state of economic misery and political distrust, surely there is a limit to just how much keeping calm and carrying on a gentleman or lady might be expected to undertake. You may very well find that getting your dander up might be the only way to get things changed around here.

To help you achieve a new state of mild motivation, *Sod Calm and Get Angry* brings together several centuries of embattled and embittered epithets. Some are from our own most clear-eyed and seasoned complainers like Benjamin Disraeli, Betrand Russell, Jonathan Swift, George Bernard Shaw. We've also combed the continent and the New World to reveal cynicism and resignation from Napoleon and Voltaire to Abraham Lincoln and Charles M Schultz. It would seem that across the world and across the centuries, there is plenty of evidence to suggest you're not alone in bemoaning the way the odds are stacked.

Fear not the cynic and the curmudgeon, for he or she is by definition not a true misanthrope, but usually a romantic in their bunker. Here is someone who is simply protecting their true ideals from the harsh realities they encounter on a daily basis. The cynic is in fact the one who cares the most. So the purpose of this collection of resigned advice is not to make you even more bitter, but maybe to offer a temporary salve in these unyielding hard times; a few well-turned grumbles and whines to help release a little pent-up steam. Perhaps these comforting negative thoughts might steer you to a more nourishing, positive future. For surely, if we manage to dodge the oncoming train, there is a sunlit end to the tunnel somewhere ahead?

POLITICS

POLITICS, N. STRIFE OF INTERESTS MASQUERADING AS A CONTEST OF PRINCIPLES. THE CONDUCT OF PUBLIC AFFAIRS FOR PRIVATE ADVANTAGE.

Ambrose Bierce

THE WORD 'POLITICS' IS DERIVED FROM THE WORD 'POLY', MEANING 'MANY', AND THE WORD 'TICKS', MEANING 'BLOOD SUCKING PARASITES'.

Larry Hardiman

MY CHOICE EARLY IN LIFE WAS EITHER TO BE A PIANO-PLAYER IN A WHOREHOUSE OR A POLITICIAN. AND TO TELL THE TRUTH, THERE'S HARDLY ANY DIFFERENCE.

Harry S Truman

**POLITICS IS
SUPPOSED TO BE
THE SECOND-OLDEST
PROFESSION. I HAVE
COME TO REALISE
THAT IT BEARS
A VERY CLOSE
RESEMBLANCE
TO THE FIRST.**

Ronald Reagan

POLITICS IS THE ART OF LOOKING FOR TROUBLE, FINDING IT, MISDIAGNOSING IT, AND THEN MISAPPLYING THE WRONG REMEDIES.

Groucho Marx

POLITICS IS PERHAPS THE ONLY PROFESSION FOR WHICH NO PREPARATION IS THOUGHT NECESSARY.

Robert Louis Stevenson

WHENEVER A MAN HAS CAST A LONGING EYE ON OFFICES, A ROTTENNESS BEGINS IN HIS CONDUCT.

Thomas Jefferson

I HAVE COME TO THE CONCLUSION THAT POLITICS ARE TOO SERIOUS A MATTER TO BE LEFT TO THE POLITICIANS.

Charles De Gaulle

POLITICIANS

WE HANG THE PETTY THIEVES AND APPOINT THE GREAT ONES TO PUBLIC OFFICE.

Aesop

HE KNOWS NOTHING AND THINKS HE KNOWS EVERYTHING. THAT POINTS CLEARLY TO A POLITICAL CAREER.

George Bernard Shaw

POLITICIANS ARE THE SAME ALL OVER. THEY PROMISE TO BUILD A BRIDGE EVEN WHERE THERE IS NO RIVER.

Nikita Khrushchev

A GOOD POLITICIAN IS QUITE AS UNTHINKABLE AS AN HONEST BURGLAR.

H L Mencken

THERE ARE NO TRUE FRIENDS IN POLITICS. WE ARE ALL SHARKS CIRCLING, AND WAITING, FOR TRACES OF BLOOD TO APPEAR IN THE WATER.

Alan Clark

INSTEAD OF GIVING A POLITICIAN THE KEYS TO THE CITY, IT MIGHT BE BETTER TO CHANGE THE LOCKS.

Doug Larson

AN HONEST POLITICIAN IS ONE WHO, WHEN HE IS BOUGHT, WILL STAY BOUGHT.

Simon Cameron

IT IS INEXCUSABLE FOR SCIENTISTS TO TORTURE ANIMALS; LET THEM MAKE THEIR EXPERIMENTS ON JOURNALISTS AND POLITICIANS.

Henrik Ibsen

A POLITICIAN IS AN ANIMAL WHO CAN SIT ON A FENCE AND YET KEEP BOTH EARS TO THE GROUND.

H L Mencken

THE ART OF
POLITICS

POLITICAL SUCCESS IS THE ABILITY, WHEN THE INEVITABLE OCCURS, TO GET CREDIT FOR IT.

Laurence J Peter

IN POLITICS ...
NEVER RETREAT,
NEVER RETRACT ...
NEVER ADMIT
A MISTAKE.

Napoleon Bonaparte

POLITICS IS THE ART OF PREVENTING PEOPLE FROM STICKING THEIR NOSES IN THINGS THAT ARE PROPERLY THEIR BUSINESS.

Paul Valéry

IF YOU CAN'T CONVINCE THEM, CONFUSE THEM.

Harry S Truman

DEMOCRACY

UNDER DEMOCRACY ONE PARTY ALWAYS DEVOTES ITS CHIEF ENERGIES TO TRYING TO PROVE THAT THE OTHER PARTY IS UNFIT TO RULE – AND BOTH COMMONLY SUCCEED, AND ARE RIGHT.

H L Mencken

**APPARENTLY,
A DEMOCRACY IS
A PLACE WHERE
NUMEROUS ELECTIONS
ARE HELD AT GREAT
COST WITHOUT
ISSUES AND WITH
INTERCHANGEABLE
CANDIDATES.**

Gore Vidal

**THE WHOLE DREAM
OF DEMOCRACY
IS TO RAISE THE
PROLETARIAN
TO THE LEVEL OF
STUPIDITY ATTAINED
BY THE BOURGEOIS.**

Gustave Flaubert

WORK

ONE OF THE SYMPTOMS OF AN APPROACHING NERVOUS BREAKDOWN IS THE BELIEF THAT ONE'S WORK IS TERRIBLY IMPORTANT.

Bertrand Russell

BY WORKING FAITHFULLY EIGHT HOURS A DAY, YOU MAY EVENTUALLY GET TO BE A BOSS AND WORK TWELVE HOURS A DAY.

Robert Frost

HARD WORK NEVER KILLED ANYBODY, BUT WHY TAKE A CHANCE?

Edgar Bergen

I LIKE WORK;
IT FASCINATES ME.
I CAN SIT AND LOOK
AT IT FOR HOURS.

Jerome K Jerome

A LIFE SPENT IN CONSTANT LABOR IS A LIFE WASTED, SAVE A MAN BE SUCH A FOOL AS TO REGARD A FULSOME OBITUARY NOTICE AS AMPLE REWARD.

George Jean Nathan

FAR FROM IDLENESS BEING THE ROOT OF ALL EVIL, IT IS RATHER THE ONLY TRUE GOOD.

Soren Kierkegaard

**A GOOD RULE
OF THUMB IS IF
YOU'VE MADE IT
TO THIRTY-FIVE
AND YOUR JOB
STILL REQUIRES
YOU TO WEAR A
NAME TAG, YOU'VE
MADE A SERIOUS
VOCATIONAL ERROR.**

Dennis Miller

THE BEST TIME TO START THINKING ABOUT YOUR RETIREMENT IS BEFORE THE BOSS DOES.

Anon

STUPIDITY

ONLY TWO THINGS ARE INFINITE, THE UNIVERSE AND HUMAN STUPIDITY, AND I'M NOT SURE ABOUT THE FORMER.

Albert Einstein

CABBAGE: A FAMILIAR KITCHEN-GARDEN VEGETABLE ABOUT AS LARGE AND WISE AS A MAN'S HEAD.

Ambrose Bierce

A GREAT MANY PEOPLE THINK THEY ARE THINKING WHEN THEY ARE MERELY REARRANGING THEIR PREJUDICES.

William James

THE ONLY REASON SOME PEOPLE GET LOST IN THOUGHT IS BECAUSE IT'S UNFAMILIAR TERRITORY.

Paul Fix

**THAT MEN
DO NOT LEARN
VERY MUCH FROM
THE LESSONS OF
HISTORY IS THE
MOST IMPORTANT
OF ALL THE LESSONS
THAT HISTORY HAS
TO TEACH.**

Aldous Huxley

THE AVERAGE MAN'S OPINIONS ARE MUCH LESS FOOLISH THAN THEY WOULD BE IF HE THOUGHT FOR HIMSELF.

Bertrand Russell

HALF THE WORLD IS COMPOSED OF IDIOTS, THE OTHER HALF OF PEOPLE CLEVER ENOUGH TO TAKE INDECENT ADVANTAGE OF THEM.

Walter Kerr

IT IS BETTER
TO KEEP YOUR
MOUTH CLOSED
AND LET PEOPLE
THINK YOU ARE
A FOOL THAN
TO OPEN IT AND
REMOVE ALL
DOUBT.

Mark Twain

WHEN A STUPID MAN IS DOING SOMETHING HE IS ASHAMED OF, HE ALWAYS DECLARES THAT IT IS HIS DUTY.

George Bernard Shaw

WISE MEN TALK BECAUSE THEY HAVE SOMETHING TO SAY; FOOLS, BECAUSE THEY HAVE TO SAY SOMETHING.

Plato

MONEY

MONEY:
THERE'S NOTHING
IN THE WORLD SO
DEMORALISING
AS MONEY.

Sophocles

NEVER SPEND YOUR MONEY BEFORE YOU HAVE IT.

Thomas Jefferson

I HAVE ENOUGH MONEY TO LAST ME THE REST OF MY LIFE, UNLESS I BUY SOMETHING.

Jackie Mason

HE THAT IS OF THE OPINION MONEY WILL DO EVERYTHING MAY WELL BE SUSPECTED OF DOING EVERYTHING FOR MONEY.

Benjamin Franklin

**NOTHING IS
AS IRRITATING
AS THE CHAP WHO
CHATS PLEASANTLY
TO YOU WHILE HE'S
OVERCHARGING YOU.**

Kin Hubbard

MANY OF THE THINGS YOU CAN COUNT, DON'T COUNT. MANY OF THE THINGS YOU CAN'T COUNT, REALLY COUNT.

Albert Einstein

**THE EASIEST
WAY FOR YOUR
CHILDREN TO LEARN
ABOUT MONEY IS
FOR YOU NOT
TO HAVE ANY.**

Katharine Whitehorn

OUR INCOMES ARE LIKE OUR SHOES; IF TOO SMALL, THEY GALL AND PINCH US; BUT IF TOO LARGE, THEY CAUSE US TO STUMBLE AND TRIP.

Charles Caleb Colton

MONEY CANNOT BUY HEALTH, BUT I'D SETTLE FOR A DIAMOND-STUDDED WHEELCHAIR.

Dorothy Parker

THE ONLY WAY NOT TO THINK ABOUT MONEY IS TO HAVE A GREAT DEAL OF IT.

Edith Wharton

WHEN YOU HAVE TOLD ANYONE YOU HAVE LEFT HIM A LEGACY THE ONLY DECENT THING TO DO IS TO DIE AT ONCE.

Samuel Butler

BUSINESS

THE FIRST RULE OF BUSINESS IS: DO OTHER MEN FOR THEY WOULD DO YOU.

Charles Dickens

IN MODERN
BUSINESS IT IS
NOT THE CROOK
WHO IS TO BE
FEARED MOST,
IT IS THE HONEST
MAN WHO DOESN'T
KNOW WHAT HE
IS DOING.

William Wordsworth

BUSINESS IS A GOOD GAME – LOTS OF COMPETITION AND A MINIMUM OF RULES. YOU KEEP SCORE WITH MONEY.

Nolan Bushnell

CRIMINAL:
A PERSON WITH
PREDATORY
INSTINCTS WHO
HAS NOT SUFFICIENT
CAPITAL TO FORM
A CORPORATION.

Howard Scott

THE DEFINITION OF A CONSULTANT: SOMEONE WHO BORROWS YOUR WATCH, TELLS YOU THE TIME AND THEN CHARGES YOU FOR THE PRIVILEGE.

A letter in The Times

NOTHING IS ILLEGAL IF A HUNDRED BUSINESSMEN DECIDE TO DO IT, AND THAT'S TRUE ANYWHERE IN THE WORLD.

Andrew Young

ADVERTISING MAY BE DESCRIBED AS THE SCIENCE OF ARRESTING THE HUMAN INTELLIGENCE LONG ENOUGH TO GET MONEY FROM IT.

Stephen Leacock

BUSINESS?
IT'S QUITE SIMPLE.
IT'S OTHER
PEOPLE'S MONEY.

Alexandre Dumas

BANKS

THEY USUALLY HAVE TWO TELLERS IN MY LOCAL BANK, EXCEPT WHEN IT'S VERY BUSY, WHEN THEY HAVE ONE.

Rita Rudner

THE MODERN
BANKING SYSTEM
MANUFACTURES MONEY
OUT OF NOTHING.
THE PROCESS IS
PERHAPS THE MOST
ASTOUNDING PIECE
OF SLEIGHT-OF-HAND
THAT WAS EVER
INVENTED. BANKING
WAS CONCEIVED IN
INEQUITY AND

**BORN IN SIN ...
BUT IF YOU WANT TO
CONTINUE TO BE SLAVES
OF THE BANKERS AND
PAY THE COST OF YOUR
OWN SLAVERY, THEN LET
THE BANKERS CONTINUE
TO CREATE MONEY AND
CONTROL CREDIT.**

Josiah Charles Stamp

FINANCE IS THE ART OF PASSING MONEY FROM HAND TO HAND UNTIL IT FINALLY DISAPPEARS.

Robert W Sarnoff

**IF YOU OWE THE
BANK $100 THAT'S
YOUR PROBLEM.
IF YOU OWE THE
BANK $100 MILLION,
THAT'S THE BANK'S
PROBLEM.**

J. Paul Getty

DEBT

**IF YOU THINK
NOBODY CARES
IF YOU'RE ALIVE,
TRY MISSING
A COUPLE OF
CAR PAYMENTS.**

Earl Wilson

MY PROBLEM LIES IN RECONCILING MY GROSS HABITS WITH MY NET INCOME.

Errol Flynn

**WE DIDN'T
ACTUALLY
OVERSPEND
OUR BUDGET.
THE ALLOCATION
SIMPLY FELL
SHORT OF OUR
EXPENDITURE.**

Keith Davis

**IT IS ONLY
BY NOT PAYING
ONE'S BILLS THAT
ONE CAN HOPE
TO LIVE IN THE
MEMORY OF THE
COMMERCIAL
CLASSES.**

Oscar Wilde

**WHEN I ASKED
MY ACCOUNTANT
IF ANYTHING COULD
GET ME OUT OF THIS
MESS I AM IN NOW,
HE THOUGHT FOR
A LONG TIME AND
SAID, 'YES, DEATH
WOULD HELP.'**

Robert Morley

A LOT OF PEOPLE BECOME PESSIMISTS FROM FINANCING OPTIMISTS.

C T Jones

A CREDITOR IS WORSE THAN A SLAVE-OWNER; FOR THE MASTER OWNS ONLY YOUR PERSON, BUT A CREDITOR OWNS YOUR DIGNITY, AND CAN COMMAND IT.

Victor Hugo

HE THAT DIES
PAYS ALL DEBTS.

William Shakespeare

THE MOMENT
YOU'RE BORN
YOU'RE DONE FOR.

Arnold Bennett

YOUTH IS
A BLUNDER;
MANHOOD A
STRUGGLE; OLD
AGE A REGRET.

Benjamin Disraeli

LIFE IS NOT SO BAD IF YOU HAVE PLENTY OF LUCK, A GOOD PHYSIQUE AND NOT TOO MUCH IMAGINATION.

Christopher Isherwood

IF YOU WAKE UP
AND YOU'RE NOT
IN PAIN, YOU KNOW
YOU'RE DEAD.

Russian proverb

THE SOONER YOU FALL BEHIND, THE MORE TIME YOU'LL HAVE TO CATCH UP!

Ogden's Law

EVERYTHING HAS BEEN FIGURED OUT, EXCEPT HOW TO LIVE.

Jean-Paul Sartre

THAT'S THE SECRET TO LIFE ... REPLACE ONE WORRY WITH ANOTHER.

Charles M Schulz

LIFE IS EASY
TO CHRONICLE,
BUT BEWILDERING
TO PRACTISE.

E M Forster

I KNOW GOD
WILL NOT GIVE
ME ANYTHING
I CAN'T HANDLE.
I JUST WISH THAT
HE DIDN'T TRUST
ME SO MUCH.

Mother Teresa

CIVILISATION

YOU CAN'T
SAY CIVILISATION
DON'T ADVANCE ...
FOR IN EVERY WAR
THEY KILL YOU
A NEW WAY.

Will Rogers

IN OUR CIVILISATION,
AND UNDER OUR
REPUBLICAN FORM
OF GOVERNMENT,
INTELLIGENCE IS
SO HIGHLY HONORED
THAT IT IS REWARDED
BY EXEMPTION FROM
THE CARES OF OFFICE.

Ambrose Bierce

IT IS PREOCCUPATION WITH POSSESSION, MORE THAN ANYTHING ELSE, THAT PREVENTS MEN FROM LIVING FREELY AND NOBLY.

Bertrand Russell

HAPPINESS

HAPPINESS, N. AN AGREEABLE SENSATION ARISING FROM CONTEMPLATING THE MISERY OF ANOTHER.

Ambrose Bierce

HAPPINESS IS A PERPETUAL POSSESSION OF BEING WELL DECEIVED.

Jonathan Swift

WE ARE MORE INTERESTED IN MAKING OTHERS BELIEVE WE ARE HAPPY THAN IN TRYING TO BE HAPPY OURSELVES.

François de La Rochefoucauld

WE WISH TO BE HAPPIER THAN OTHER PEOPLE; AND THIS IS ALWAYS DIFFICULT, FOR WE BELIEVE OTHERS TO BE HAPPIER THAN THEY ARE.

Charles-Louis de Secondat
baron de Montesquieu

**POINT ME OUT
THE HAPPY MAN
AND I WILL
POINT YOU OUT
EITHER EGOTISM,
SELFISHNESS,
EVIL – OR ELSE
AN ABSOLUTE
IGNORANCE.**

Graham Greene

WHAT A WONDERFUL LIFE I'VE HAD! I ONLY WISH I'D REALISED IT SOONER.

Colette

I'M AN OPTIMIST, BUT I'M AN OPTIMIST WHO CARRIES A RAINCOAT.

Harold Wilson

CALL NO MAN
HAPPY TILL
HE IS DEAD.

Aeschylus

UNHAPPINESS

MEN WHO
ARE UNHAPPY,
LIKE MEN WHO
SLEEP BADLY,
ARE ALWAYS PROUD
OF THE FACT.

Bertrand Russell

ASK YOURSELF WHETHER YOU ARE HAPPY, AND YOU CEASE TO BE SO.

John Stuart Mill

NOBODY REALLY CARES IF YOU'RE MISERABLE, SO YOU MIGHT AS WELL BE HAPPY.

Cynthia Nelms

AND YET TO EVERY BAD THERE IS A WORSE.

Thomas Hardy

DECEIT

WHEN WE ASK FOR ADVICE, WE ARE USUALLY LOOKING FOR AN ACCOMPLICE.

Marquis de la Grange

A GOVERNMENT THAT ROBS PETER TO PAY PAUL CAN ALWAYS DEPEND ON THE SUPPORT OF PAUL.

George Bernard Shaw

IT IS ALWAYS
THE BEST POLICY
TO SPEAK THE
TRUTH – UNLESS,
OF COURSE, YOU ARE
AN EXCEPTIONALLY
GOOD LIAR.

Jerome K Jerome

LYING IS DONE WITH WORDS AND ALSO WITH SILENCE.

Adrienne Rich

HOW FORTUNATE FOR LEADERS THAT MEN DO NOT THINK.

Adolf Hitler

HYPOCRISY

**HYPOCRITE:
THE MAN WHO
MURDERED BOTH
HIS PARENTS ...
PLEADED FOR
MERCY ON THE
GROUNDS THAT HE
WAS AN ORPHAN.**

Abraham Lincoln

LET US BE GRATEFUL TO THE MIRROR FOR REVEALING TO US OUR APPEARANCE ONLY.

Samuel Butler

THE TRUE HYPOCRITE IS THE ONE WHO CEASES TO PERCEIVE HIS DECEPTION, THE ONE WHO LIES WITH SINCERITY.

André Gide

MORALITY

IT'S DISCOURAGING TO THINK HOW MANY PEOPLE ARE SHOCKED BY HONESTY AND HOW FEW BY DECEIT.

Noël Coward

WE HAVE, IN FACT, TWO KINDS OF MORALITY SIDE BY SIDE: ONE WHICH WE PREACH BUT DO NOT PRACTISE AND ANOTHER WHICH WE PRACTISE BUT SELDOM PREACH.

Bertrand Russell

I HATE MANKIND,
FOR I THINK
MYSELF ONE OF
THE BEST OF THEM,
AND I KNOW HOW
BAD I AM.

Joseph Baretti

THE MODERN CONSERVATIVE IS ENGAGED IN ONE OF MAN'S OLDEST EXERCISES IN MORAL PHILOSOPHY; THAT IS, THE SEARCH FOR A SUPERIOR MORAL JUSTIFICATION FOR SELFISHNESS.

J K Galbraith

RAT RACE

NEVER KEEP UP WITH THE JONESES. DRAG THEM DOWN TO YOUR LEVEL. IT'S CHEAPER.

Quentin Crisp

YOU CAN NEVER GET ENOUGH OF WHAT YOU DON'T NEED TO MAKE YOU HAPPY.

Eric Hoffer

NOTHING AGES
YOUR CAR AS MUCH
AS THE SIGHT OF
YOUR NEIGHBOR'S
NEW ONE.

Evan Esar

THE WORLD IS FULL
OF FOOLS AND FAINT
HEARTS; AND YET
EVERYONE HAS
COURAGE ENOUGH
TO BEAR THE
MISFORTUNES, AND
WISDOM ENOUGH TO
MANAGE THE AFFAIRS,
OF HIS NEIGHBOR.

Benjamin Franklin

WHENEVER A FRIEND SUCCEEDS, A LITTLE SOMETHING IN ME DIES.

Gore Vidal

CURMUDGEON

START OFF
EVERY DAY WITH
A SMILE AND GET
IT OVER WITH.

W C Fields

THE FIRST HALF OF OUR LIVES IS RUINED BY OUR PARENTS, AND THE SECOND HALF BY OUR CHILDREN.

Clarence Darrow

I HAVE ALWAYS DISLIKED MYSELF AT ANY GIVEN MOMENT; THE TOTAL OF SUCH MOMENTS IS MY LIFE.

Cyril Connolly

**PATIENCE, N.
A MINOR FORM
OF DESPAIR,
DISGUISED AS
A VIRTUE.**

Ambrose Bierce

A CYNIC IS A MAN WHO, WHEN HE SMELLS FLOWERS, LOOKS AROUND FOR A COFFIN.

H L Mencken

ANGER

IN CERTAIN TRYING
CIRCUMSTANCES,
URGENT
CIRCUMSTANCES,
DESPERATE
CIRCUMSTANCES,
PROFANITY
FURNISHES A
RELIEF DENIED
EVEN TO PRAYER.

Mark Twain

NEVER GO
TO BED MAD.
STAY UP
AND FIGHT.

Phyllis Diller

**SPEAK WHEN
YOU ARE ANGRY
AND YOU WILL
MAKE THE BEST
SPEECH YOU WILL
EVER REGRET.**

Ambrose Bierce

PROTEST

THERE MAY BE TIMES WHEN WE ARE POWERLESS TO PREVENT INJUSTICE, BUT THERE MUST NEVER BE A TIME WHEN WE FAIL TO PROTEST.

Elie Wiesel

**THE WORLD
IS A DANGEROUS
PLACE, NOT BECAUSE
OF THOSE WHO DO
EVIL, BUT BECAUSE
OF THOSE WHO
LOOK ON AND
DO NOTHING.**

Albert Einstein

WE MUST NOT ALLOW OURSELVES TO BECOME LIKE THE SYSTEM WE OPPOSE.

Archbishop Desmond Tutu

YOU MUST
DO THE THINGS
YOU THINK YOU
CANNOT DO.

Eleanor Roosevelt

**NEVER DOUBT THAT
A SMALL GROUP
OF THOUGHTFUL,
COMMITTED CITIZENS
CAN CHANGE THE
WORLD. INDEED,
IT IS THE ONLY
THING THAT
EVER HAS.**

Margaret Mead

TOO CROSS TO
THINK STRAIGHT?
YOU NEED: